STAND OUT
COVER LETTERS

How to Write Winning
Cover Letters That Get You Hired

Mark Baker

ISBN: 9781520127729

Legal Notice

Please note that much of the information in this book is based on personal experience that has worked for the author. You should use this information as you see fit and at your own risk. Your particular circumstances may not be exactly the same, and you should adjust your use of the information accordingly. Use your own best judgement in all situations. Nothing in this book is intended to replace legal/professional advice.

Please note some of the links in this book may be affiliate links. If you click them and buy something, I may be paid a commission, with no extra cost to you. I only include links to my own products or services or to products or services that I have used or would happily use.

The author acknowledges the trademarked status and trademark owners of the following trademarks mentioned in this work of non-fiction:

Google: Google Inc., Post-it: Post-it Notes, Facebook: Facebook Inc., Ford Motor Company, SurveyMonkey, Preptel

Dedication

To all people everywhere who are ready to stand up, stand out and do things differently.

Acknowledgements

My family and friends have always encouraged me to stand out. Thank you for always believing in me no matter what.

Chandler Bolt and the wonderful team and community at "Self Publishing School". Thank you for 'holding my hand' throughout the writing and publishing process.

Everyone else who assisted me with preparing this book for publication: Candela Iglesias Chiesa, my writing buddy who kept me sane when I was sure I was losing it, Jyotsna Ramachandran and her team at Happy Self Publishing, for creating the cover, my editor, Miranda Regan, as well as my wonderful launch team. Without all of you this book would never have come to be. Thank you.

Download your FREE Workbook

Increase your chances of writing a great cover letter by using the workbook while reading this book. You can download the workbook for free by going to the link below:

http://www.thestandoutway.com/stand-out-cover-letters-workbook-download

Table of Contents

Chapter 1:

STAND OUT OR MISS OUT

If you've ever applied for a job only to never hear a word back, you'll know exactly how disheartening this silent rejection can be. The fact is it's becoming increasingly difficult to get noticed in the overcrowded job market. Basically every job gets far too many applications.

Technology makes it easy for companies to post their job openings to a mass audience, which means they can potentially reach a larger target market, and that means more competition for every job. Technology also makes it easy for that larger target market to apply for jobs regardless of whether they're a good match or not. Many people apply for jobs they should never have applied for in the first place.

Recruiters, hiring managers and their personal assistants are bombarded with far more applications than they have time to read. No wonder they've had to become ruthless cullers in an attempt to find the best candidates for the job.

Remember too that the chief culler or gatekeeper sometimes takes the form of an even more unforgiving agent—the dreaded Applicant Tracking System (ATS). This is automated software used by most large companies to screen out candidates long before human eyes ever see an application.

Fail to move past any of these pre-screening checkpoints and you won't even get an interview. Without an interview, you'll lose any opportunity to convince a potential employer that you're the one for the job. End of story. The message to job seekers is simple—stand out or you'll miss out. But how?

The Solution

What's the solution to this problem? How can you stand out from your peers? By taking advantage of an often marginalized element of the application package: the cover letter.

Often applications start with no cover letters or they are either too generic, add no value at all or look no different to any of their competitors' letters. In short you need to learn how to write a letter of introduction that's impossible ignore.

First impressions count for a lot, especially when it comes to applying for jobs. A cover letter designed to have you stand out from the rest is the perfect vehicle to help you make a great first impression fast. And fast you'd better be, because you'll only have seconds in which to accomplish this. Get it right though and you'll showcase your personality and unique qualities in such a way that recruiters and hiring managers will be excited and eager to meet you.

I'm not talking about just any cover letter and definitely nothing like the ones you've written before—if you have. Rather, this will be a newly-repurposed, dynamic and devilishly well-crafted piece of marketing that will grab people's attention and fast track you all the way into your dream job. This book will show you exactly how to create such a cover letter.

But Does Anybody Read Them?

Wait, I'm suggesting you write a cover letter, but you may have heard that no one reads cover letters these days, so why should you even bother? I've seen the statistics used to support this idea, but I've never heard it said that you shouldn't include a cover letter unless a company requests you leave it out. Could it be that more letters would be read if they actually stood out from the rest?

I'm not alone in believing cover letters still have a place in the application process. I searched for the term, 'cover letter' on Google and got 109,000,000 entries. Okay, so it's not as popular a term as 'sex and the city' (698,000,000), but I'd say more than a hundred million entries is enough to declare that cover letters are still among the living.

Isn't a Resume More Important?

But what about a resume? Isn't it more important? In one word, no! Having a relevant and tailored resume is important but leave out a compelling cover letter and you'll miss out on one of the most potent marketing opportunities available to you as a job seeker. A resume by nature can't be as dynamic as a cover letter can be. Resumes are deigned to list relevant information as succinctly and effectively as possible, period.

Cover letters, on the other hand, don't have to just be a list of facts. They can be bold, sizzling, unexpected, full of personality and impossible to ignore. If cover letters are being ignored, it's because most aren't worth reading.

Why Should You Listen to me?

Because I've had plenty of experience, however, I'm not a recruitment guru nor do I profess to know everything there is to know about this subject. But I've applied for and been accepted for more jobs across a wider range of interests than the average person. That means I've written a lot of cover letters.

To name just some of my previous roles - I've worked as a school teacher, on board luxury passenger liners, in sales, corporate training, hospitality, in tourism, as a cleaner, barman, and fitness instructor. Not only have I written many cover letters but I've perfected the art of writing these to get the jobs I want.

On the flip side, many of my roles have required me to hire others. Working for a number of global companies has afforded me the opportunity to collaborate with other hiring managers and talent acquisition teams, so I'm also well up on what impresses on the other end.

But don't take my word for it, take what I teach for a ride and prove it to yourself. What matters is that it works, not for me, but for you.

What to Expect

What I already know about writing a stand out cover letter I believe anybody can learn. You too have the potential to market yourself effectively; you simply have to learn how to do it. To do this, you'll need to go through a simple process that is about far more than just learning the mechanics of how to write a letter.

To write an authentic cover letter that stands out, you must want to stand out as a candidate, know why you do, believe that you do and be able to project this first as person and then in your letter. This is not about cutting and pasting words from sterile templates or writing letters that follow useless, outdated guidelines. This is about you making a decision to stand up and stand out by owning your future. Are you ready to do that? If you are, this book can help.

First, I'm going to ask you to make a conscious decision about whether you want to stand out. If you decide yes, then you'll be ready to be different and, concerning cover letters at least, to do things differently. Deciding to stand out is easy, but being prepared for what may follow can be difficult. Be assured, I'll help you to prepare for the journey ahead so you'll always feel ready to move to the next step

Once you decide to stand out, we'll dive right in and revamp the old cover letter idea. That way you'll know from the beginning what you're working towards. You'll discover why cover letters of the past will no longer work for this new stand out you. We'll give an outdated concept a total overhaul, giving you the foundation you need to create a letter that will 'sell' you as the perfect candidate to any employer.

Then I'll help you know your own value. Even if, right now, you think you have little to offer. After this I'll have you do a quick check of your perspective to make sure you're viewing yourself not as just another job applicant but as the total solution to a company's needs.

Once that's done, you'll be ready to determine whether the job you're considering really is the job for you. When you're sure that it is, you'll move on to learning how to write your new and improved letter step-by-step.

In short, this book will bring you to a place where you can craft a cover letter that's been thoroughly re-invented for today, ready to achieve its objective like an on-target missile. With this cover letter, you can get your dream job, earn what you're worth and more importantly, grow further in your professional life and be happy while you're doing it.

I can't guarantee that every one of your cover letters will be read, but I can show you how to craft a letter that, if it is, will help you stand out from the pack. I'll also reveal how you can use your new and revived cover letter to get interviews for the 80% of jobs never advertised, known as the hidden job market.

In addition, I'll let you in on some obvious, but usually overlooked, packaging and delivery secrets, one of which has nothing at all to do with letter writing. In fact this one idea will almost certainly increase the chances of you standing out. You do also need to know how to write a cover letter for both human and bot (ATS) eyes. This book will show you how to do both.

What's more, when you know how to write a cover letter as I'll teach you, you'll also know how to present yourself when you come face-to-face with your interviewers. Learning how to write a cover letter for today's job market is about adopting a specific mindset. Once you have this in place, you'll carry it with you throughout your application journey.

This Book Has Already Helped Many Job Seekers Just Like You

What you'll learn here has already been tested and proved. Much of the information in this book I've been sharing with friends and coaching students for a while. One such person is Tammy from London. She had been trying to move from being a teacher to a customer service trainer, but she never seemed to progress to the interview stage. She asked me to take a look at her application.

Straight away I could see how her cover letter was letting her down. She was making a big mistake but a common one. Her letter screamed that she didn't have much customer service experience when in fact all she needed to do was 'join the dots' between her teaching experience and the new job requirements. With her letter tweaked and rewritten following the same simple format I'll teach you later, she started applying for more jobs. Not only did she get call-backs, interviews and, eventually, a job she wanted, but employers made special mention to her about her cover letters.

What About You?

You too can be like Tammy. Follow the step-by-step process in this book, and I promise you'll not only feel like you're more in control of your application, but you'll also start to see a dramatic increase in the number of positive responses. You may not always get the job, but if you have the resume and interview skills to match your cover letter, you can be a serious contender for the job of your dreams.

You can be the person who immediately and unexpectedly stands out to future employers. You can be the person who gets the phone call inviting you to interviews. You can be the person who they're excited to meet and who they're sure they want working for them. You can be the person who gets all the best jobs because you know how to make it happen.

Are You Ready to Be Successful?

All you need to be successful is to be willing and ready to read and put into action what you're about to learn here as soon as possible. Failure to act is another wasted day, another missed opportunity, another job you could have interviewed for, another day when someone else perhaps not nearly as suitable as you gets the job that should have been yours.

This is a book for serious job seekers. It's for people who want to stand out by contributing and growing meaningfully in their work places. It's for people who want to be in the right job, happy and fulfilled, and who want to know how to write a cover letter that will get them there.

No matter whether you're a new graduate, an experienced senior executive or midway through your career and thinking of changing industries, this book can help you. Expect to find help here, and you very probably will.

But if you're only interested in getting a job, any job,

just so you can pay the bills, then this book isn't for you. You'd be better off cutting and pasting from the sterile letter templates available for free online.

What if you're not in any of the specific industries I'm going to cover? Just because your industry or specific situation is not covered doesn't mean the same principles don't apply. What you may need to do is adapt what you read for your specific needs. If you find yourself thinking that something doesn't apply to you, stop and ask, '*So what? How can I make this work for me and my situation?*' Let your mind work and dig up some ideas. Set yourself up to be successful rather than looking for reasons why you should fail.

This isn't the only book ever written on this subject. This isn't the only way to write a cover letter. However, you're here right now, reading *this* book so I want to encourage you to be open to what it teaches so that you can get the most from it.

So are you ready to stand out and learn how to write winning cover letters that get you hired? If the answer is yes, congratulations, it's time to start the process that will take you by the hand and lead you towards being the stand out success that you can be.

Chapter 2:

PREPARE TO STAND OUT

So you've decided to stand out. Well done! But as I said before, making this decision is the easy part, dealing with the taunting emotions that could follow, not that much fun. In my opinion it's best to be as prepared as possible so you can tackle these when they come up. In this chapter, I'll help you equip yourself for the way ahead.

Understanding How We Operate

Even though you have decided you want to stand out you need to know that for most of us this goes against what comes naturally to us. As humans, we're not programmed to stand out. In fact, we're more likely to try to blend in as much as possible. Sure, you might be desperate to be noticed, but only to fit in and feel like you belong. Ironic, isn't it?

The good news is that you're not broken. Most human beings default to conformity. We want to be the same and do the same things as everybody else. We may be more evolved than our animal friends in some ways, but at this basic level there's no difference. Like them we are still gregarious. 'Gregarious' comes from the Latin word 'grex', meaning herd or flock. We like to move together because it gives us a sense of belonging.

Conforming is the exact opposite of standing out. To some extent, we're all conformists. Observe the clothes we wear and the styles of cars, houses, food and travel we choose. All often similar. Conforming can be beneficial; it strengthens our sense of belonging. It's not always useful though when we want to get ahead in life and escape the pack.

When conformity restricts your personal growth and leads to frustration and unhappiness, then it's hazardous. So what does this mean in the context of writing cover letters?

Without even realizing, you've probably been holding yourself back, conforming to limitations, writing cover letters that are so safe and similar to everybody else's that yours have been overlooked time and time again, just like theirs have been overlooked.

Conforming could mean you've lost out on jobs you wanted or that you've ended up in jobs you later discovered you never wanted in the first place, cycles you repeat over and over again. Consider how much of your life you'll spend working. Conformity can mean a life that is, for the most part, unhappy and unfulfilled. But it doesn't have to be this way.

Breaking Free from Sameness

You can break free from conformity. To do this, you must first become aware that you've been conforming and that doing so hasn't got you what you want. Then you have to make a decision to stand out instead. I

11

know since you've read this far you've probably already made that decision. Once you make the decision to stand out, you declare that you're going to go against what everybody else is doing and try something different. In other words, *change*. This is where problems usually start.

We Don't Like Change

Change is hard. We become comfortable conforming. It's a safe, familiar way of life, and our mind regards anything that threatens this safety as an enemy, to be stopped in any way possible. For this reason, we're resistant to change. To stand out you must change by developing and expressing your individuality, which means you'll probably feel insecure, vulnerable and 'not right'. And because we hate feeling these emotions, most of the time we would rather slip back to conforming.

Recognizing and Dealing with the Signs

The key is to recognize these feelings. When you can identify the signs that signal resistance, then you'll be better able to deal with them accordingly. Basically any negative feelings spawned by your change in mindset are a sign that you want to resist the change.

In this book, you'll be looking at yourself and asking what makes you stand out as a human being and, more specifically, as an employee. Hopefully, it makes sense that you can only write a stand out cover letter if what it represents is a stand out future employee.

You may find it challenging to acknowledge who you are and what you're good at. Your mind will tell you all kinds of bogus stories like 'I can't think of anything to write. It's a silly exercise. I'm too tired to do this' etc. When thoughts like these come up, catch yourself and laugh at your mind. Tell it to take a hike. Ask, *So what?* Be prepared to push through until you're done.

Further on, you'll be learning about a different approach to writing cover letters. Don't be surprised if you have doubts about whether the information is correct and trustworthy. You see, your mind would rather protect you by suggesting that you're better off with what you know.

Again it's simply a matter of being aware of your emotions and thoughts. You need to recognize that having them doesn't mean they're accurate or valid.

If you discuss what you read in this book with others, they may disagree with you and discourage you from taking such a little-trodden path. Their disagreement may make you feel uneasy, but recognize it as another sign. None of us want to feel that we're wrong. To have others, especially those whose opinions we value, think we're wrong is sometimes too much for us to deal with. Also, realize that sometimes people reject the new paths of others because they're afraid they'll find out *they* are the ones on the wrong path.

Think of it this way: who says there's only one right way to do anything? Wouldn't you be better being certain by following through to the end to find out? What's the worst that can happen? If you do find yourself in this situation, allow others to have their opinion, but self-talk yourself into staying with the process. Remember what I said about why it's important for you to test this for yourself. Nobody but you can do this.

Emotional Management

How well you can manage your emotions when they signal danger will determine how skilled you become at dealing with resistance to change. Sometimes you'll do well. Sometimes you'll be caught off guard. The secret lies in continually developing your awareness and practicing ways of not letting your crafty mind trick you.

To stand out takes the courage and determination to overcome your inevitable resistance to change. But it's possible, and you can do it. Fearing change will strengthen your resistance so, at every opportunity, celebrate your decision to be different. Do this and you will finally be giving the real you an opportunity to emerge.

Reason with yourself when feelings of resistance come up. Remind yourself that you made a decision to stand out because deep down you value your individuality and creative potential. To succeed you must have a burning desire to rise above the crowd. Why do you have this? What is it that you want to change? Is it important to you? Why? If you don't stand out and do things differently what will the consequences be? Will that worry you? Why?

Take responsibility for daring to be different. Don't let your mind kidnap your goal to stand out. Tell yourself 'I choose to stand out', 'I can do this', 'I will do this', 'I am doing this', 'I am the boss not my mind'.

When your mind comes up with reasons why you should return to the 'tried and tested' ways of doing things, stop and ask, 'Who says?' or 'So what?' Then simply be quiet and wait to hear your inner wisdom speak up. Most times your noisy mind will scamper off and make itself scarce, but it won't be gone for long. You must learn to become vigilant at all costs.

Finally regard what you're going to encounter here as a temporary personal experiment. You have to keep going because you won't know if it's worked until you reach the end. Often your mind will try and trick you into believing this new way will last forever with no way out. This is simply not true. You're in charge, and you always have choices.

Now that you know what to expect and how to deal with any of your mind's demonstrations against standing out, it's time to move on and give the old cover letter a new lease on life.

Chapter 3:

REPURPOSE YOUR COVER LETTER

By the end of this chapter the cover letter as you know it will be gone. In its place will rise a marketing tool designed to help you get what you want, your dream job.

Before you learn how to write a stand out cover letter, you must be clear about its purpose. Only when you understand this will you know how to write a great letter. Even though cover letters do already have an established purpose, it's an ineffective one. This doesn't mean however that you can't change this. This is what we're about to do next and it's pivotal to everything that follows.

What Does Repurpose Mean?

To repurpose means to take something designed for one purpose and recycle it for a new and improved purpose. Let me give you an example:

Recently, I was looking for a pen and pencil holder for my desk. I looked at many of these in stationery stores, but I didn't like any of them. One morning, while waiting for an appointment in one of my favourite cafés, I happened to be drinking commercially-bottled water. Suddenly, I had a flash of inspiration. What if I just cut the plastic bottle in half? I'd have an unconventional but usable pen and pencil holder.

So I did, and I love it. It's functional, interesting, and unobtrusive, plus it only cost me the price of a bottle of water. Another good thing is at least one plastic bottle, or half of one anyway, didn't make its way to the garbage dump.

So something that started out as a plastic bottle to hold water has been repurposed as a plastic container to hold pens and pencils. Amazing how repurposing something so simple can end up being so fulfilling. What if we could work the same magic with cover letters? That's exactly what we're going to do.

The Original Purpose of Cover Letters

Where did the idea of writing a cover letter come from anyway? Look up its definition in just about any dictionary and you'll more than likely find a reference back to the British. The definitions all say much the same thing—it's a letter sent with another document or parcel explaining the contents of said document or parcel.

It's no secret that, historically, the British upper class had a reputation for being overly polite and formal. Over time many of these mannerisms dripped down to the lower British classes too. Idiosyncrasies such as these were regarded as evidence of good manners, being proper and posh, even if this was far from the case.

The influence of the British Empire stretched far and wide, which meant that people all over the world adopted what was regarded as correct and expected. One of these expected bits of etiquette was the cover letter. At that time and, possibly even now, including a letter with another document or parcel can be useful if you need to explain what's in the package.

When snail mail was the norm and you applied for a job, it also made good sense to include a letter to provide more information about what was in the envelope. Take the Ford Motor Company for example. As a major employer it's likely they would have had any number of job openings available at the same time. Imagine the chaos in their HR department if they'd received only resumes stuffed into envelopes. They would have no idea what positions were being applied for without a letter to explain.

Fast forward to today when the vast majority of job applications are processed via online job sites and an explanatory letter is quite unnecessary. These days when you click on an advertised job link and apply, the advertiser knows exactly what job you're applying for. This is all connected behind the scenes. The question then is why do many employers still expect a cover letter and why do job applicants feel the need to send one?

It's probably a case of old habits die hard. Job seekers have been led to believe or even outright taught that they should send cover letters, and employers have been conditioned to expect them. But, written based on their original purpose, cover letters are completely redundant, which is why they're so often overlooked.

How Job Seekers Became Confused

Cover letters have however evolved somewhat beyond simply announcing what's in an envelope, presumably because their writers realized they had to give these required documents more of a purpose. This is where the confusion started about what you should include in such a letter.

Somewhere along the way job seekers started adding content to these letters, and this practice continues today. You may have done it yourself.

There are two common ways to add content to a cover letter. First, there's what I call the 'resume dump', where you just lift sections from your resume and insert them into your letter. Typically, these refer to your most recent experience and general skills profile. I'm sure you can work this out for yourself, but there's no point in duplicating your resume. I'm not exactly sure why you'd choose to do this. Maybe you believe you stand twice the chance of having your appropriateness for the role noticed? From experience the exact opposite occurs—the letter and resume are discarded.

Second, you may have read somewhere that a cover letter is an opportunity to market yourself. In essence, this is true, but what does it mean? Without knowing, you write paragraphs about why you think the company is a perfect match for you, why they need you and why you possess everything they could possibly be looking for in a candidate.

While your intention might be genuine, empty statements about why you think you're wonderful are meaningless and reveal more about your lack of written communication skills than anything else.

Is it any wonder job seekers like you have been confused about what to include in cover letters? You realize their original purpose is no longer valid, but deep down you also sense that filling them with fluff content isn't working either, otherwise you would not be reading this book.

From Cover to Sales

What if you took the old cover letter concept turned it on its head and repurposed it as a sales letter designed to hook your audience from the get-go? What if such a letter was able to influence readers so easily that there was no doubt in their heads that you were the one they wanted to pursue? What if this letter was so different from anyone else's cover letter that you automatically stood out as the candidate of choice? This is exactly what a cleverly crafted sales letter will achieve.

Instead of describing the contents of your application as of old or doubling up on your resume, your cover letter should be about sales. You, like many job seekers, probably don't think of getting a job as a sales transaction but this is exactly the approach you must take.

Since you're going to sell yourself, it's useful think of yourself and what you have to offer as a product and service and the potential employer as a purchaser. When you write a cover letter, what you want to do is sell yourself as a product and service that matches their needs.

If the idea of sales and selling yourself is ringing alarm

bells, don't worry! You don't have to be a professional salesperson or become anything like your idea of a stereotypical salesperson. You simply have to learn how to actively and deliberately sell yourself when you apply for a job.

A new and repurposed cover letter is the ideal vehicle for selling yourself. All that's needed is for you to implement a basic sales approach in your cover letter, which this book will teach you how to do.

If you regard yourself as 'non-salesy' and still feel absolutely terrified at the thought of having to write a sales letter, it's time to put this self-limiting idea to bed. I'm going to break it all down for you to make it easy for you to understand. When I'm done, you might wonder why you never thought of this before. This method is more about knowing and understanding the mechanics of what gets people's attention and what leads them to make decisions. It's got more to do with psychology than anything else.

So the old cover letter has been redefined and repurposed as a sales letter. I will often refer to it as such from now on. It will effectively sell you and what you can offer. If you manage to do a good job, your cover letter, not your resume, will be the thing that makes them want to meet you. Now you need to figure out what makes you stand out as a product and service so you can communicate this to your advantage when you write your letter.

Chapter 4:

DEFINE YOUR VALUE

So you've decided you want to stand out and the way in which you'll communicate this to potential employers is by writing a repurposed cover letter that follows a sales letter format. Before you can write such a letter you need to be quite clear about what makes you stand out. Note, I didn't say *if* you stand out but rather *what* makes you stand out.

You possess value exactly as you are today, right now. You just need to recognize it so you can package it in the best way possible when you write your letter. In this chapter you're going to become clear about what makes you stand out.

You may even think you don't have much to offer others, but that's only because you hardly ever take the time to fully take stock of yourself, to understand who you are and what makes you valuable. No two people are the same. Nobody else has lived and experienced life exactly as you have. Your personal profile is one of a kind.

I have no doubt you have plenty attributes that make you 'hot property', you just need to drill down and find out exactly what they are. You don't have to complete an assessment of your value every time you apply for a job, but you should work through it at least once. Then you can keep adding to it as your career progresses.

Becoming Clear about What Value Means

What makes something or someone have value? As discussed in the previous chapter, you're selling yourself as a product and service to a potential employer. In effect, you're the product or service and the salesperson all wrapped up in one. Before a salesperson can sell anything, however, they have to have a thorough understanding of what they're selling and also be super clear about the value the product or service offers. They need to know this so they can match this to the buyer's needs.

Think back to the last big purchase you made. You only handed over your cash or card once you knew what you were getting would fulfil your needs and had sufficient value. An employer won't hire you until they know the same things about you.

In 'sales-speak' the value of a product or service is often referred to as the 'features and benefits'. A feature describes some aspect of the product or service and the benefit explains why the feature is valuable. Here's an example: *This ball glows in the dark so you can play ball games outside at night.*

The ball's feature is it glows in the dark. A benefit of this feature is you can play ball games outside at night.

Every feature has to have a benefit otherwise what's the point of it? The value is in the stated benefit.

What you'll be doing in this chapter is figuring out your features and benefits so that you can communicate them to employers. You may never have thought of yourself as a product or service before, but it's helpful if you do. Of course you're far more than an inanimate item on a shelf. Your value comes from a variety of sources—your personality, qualifications, skills, achievements, experience, goals, dreams and aspirations.

The 'So What?' Question

People can often list features quite easily, but find it more challenging to determine the benefits of those features. I've found that an easy way to ascertain the benefit of any feature is to ask, *'So what?'*.

'The ball glows in the dark.' (Feature)

'So what?'

'It means you can play games in the dark.' (Benefit)

'So what?' is a question you'll see used frequently in this book. In fact, I've already used it several times. I like it because it cheekily prompts you to qualify and clarify the significance or insignificance of something. It's a question that helps you magically move from grey to full colour. In other words, it can help you find the stand out quality of something or someone.

For example, if I asked you what you did for a living and you replied, *'I'm a plumber.'* I could then ask, *'So what?'* Hundreds and thousands of people are plumbers. What makes you different? Why should I call you over anybody else? What makes you good or special? What makes you stand out?

If on the other hand you had replied, *'I help men and women in my neighbourhood have peace of mind whenever they have a plumbing emergency.'* Well now I know a whole lot more about you. In fact, you sound like a stand out plumber and, if I needed one, you'd be top of my list.

Ask 'So what?' often and sincerely. It will help you think and act differently—to stand out. You'll be applying this question a lot in the activities ahead.

Getting Feedback from Others

The first part of this exercise involves canvassing feedback from other people. This task is often referred to as a 360-degree assessment, a process where you receive confidential, anonymous feedback from the people who currently or recently worked with you.

If you don't have few people you are comfortable asking to do this, you can also approach personal friends. Remember, however, the closer people are to you the more biased they will be in your favour. They can't help being biased. They're your friends, and they like and want to support you. While your ego may like what they have to say, the objective of this exercise is honest feedback so that you can learn more about yourself.

Ideally the best people to approach are your current manager, peers, direct reports and possibly some work friends. The fact that this exercise will be anonymous and confidential should ensure that people feel more comfortable about being honest with their responses.

Also note a percentage of people will choose not to participate so always ask more people than you actually require. There's no ideal number. I'd say around fifteen people is a good target. Even if only half respond, you should get some useful feedback.

Setting Up Other People's Feedback

To collect feedback, it's best to use an online service. I recommend SurveyMonkey. They have a free and paid option, but you don't need to use the paid version. If you want to know precisely how to set up your survey, download the workbook that goes with this book. You'll find a step-by-step set of instructions with images.

Once you've created your survey, you'll send your target recipients an email either from within SurveyMonkey or from your own email account. Here is an example you could use:

Hi,

I'm currently completing a self-assessment exercise as part of a book I'm reading.

I require some quick feedback from people who know me, and I was hoping you'd be able to help me out.

If you're willing and able, please complete a short anonymous and confidential survey by [date] to give me some feedback about myself and my work habits. It would be most appreciated.

Here are some sample questions to use for your survey:

1. In the context of work, please write down 3-5 of my strengths.

2. What 3-5 personal qualities do I have that would make me an asset to an employer?

3. What 3-5 areas would you say I could work on improving?

Make sure to set a deadline. Seven days is usually sufficient. Once the deadline has expired, check your responses. Make a note of what people had to say, either on a piece of paper or in the workbook provided for download.

Whenever I do this exercise I'm always surprised by some of the responses I receive, both positive and negative. Remember that feedback is just that, another person's opinion. If nothing else, those opinions might be interesting and worth a little time exploring.

I suggest you complete this section straight away so that by the time you've finished reading and completing the other activities you'll have your responses back from your survey.

Self-Assessment

Once you've collected feedback from others, you'll need to perform a self-assessment. The word self-assessment sounds heavy and exhausting, but it doesn't have to be. The activities ahead are quite a lot of fun and creative too. Make sure you have as much fun with this as possible. It's all about discovering who you are and why you're such a stand out candidate.

Brainstorm

One of the best ways to get information out of your head and on to paper is to 'brain dump' or brainstorm the topic. There's a certain way to do this, and it only works if you follow the instructions exactly. When you do, you'll allow your brain to come up with ideas without your in-built censor judging whether something is useful or not.

In the middle of a sheet of paper, either write your name or draw a quick self-portrait to represent yourself as the main topic. Set a timer for three minutes on your watch, phone or computer. Now write down absolutely every and anything that comes to mind about yourself until the timer beeps.

Your words or ideas may sound odd or useless, but just keep writing and don't stop to think. One word will spur the next one and so on. Avoid making lists of words rather than writing the words randomly on the page around the centre point.

These words can be things you like or dislike about yourself, things others say about you, skills, experience, jobs, values—anything at all. Don't stop writing while the timer is on, and don't stop to think about or judge anything that comes up. There's no right or wrong here. You'll decide later what you can and can't use.

After the three minutes is up, you'll have a page full of random information about yourself. It'll be quite disorganized. That's fine. If you feel you didn't get enough down, you can always set another three minutes on the timer. A second round should be more than enough time to complete this part.

Personally, I like using big sheets of paper and markers when I brainstorm, but you don't have to do this. Oddly the large sheets seem to jog my brain better. You could also use a whiteboard. If you do, take a photo of it to use in the future.

Another way to do this exercise is with sticky notes. Write a different word/idea on each note and place it around a central topic note. Remember you're not organizing anything at this stage, just getting the ideas down.

You can also do this digitally, but it's been suggested that brainstorms are more effective if they're handwritten. I've certainly found this to be the case. Once again, this exercise is covered in the workbook, where I've added visuals and left you space to complete the activities.

Mind Map

Now you're going to use your 'brain dump' or brainstorm to organize similar information under headings by creating a mind map. As implied by the word 'map', it's a more directional and catalogued document. In short, it's a visual representation of your information set out in an ordered, graphical way.

Mind maps come in many 'flavours', as you'll see if you search for the term online. You'll also find some examples in the workbook.

Here are the basics: on a new sheet of paper, once again write your name in the middle or draw a self-portrait. Draw some lines extending out from the centre point. Each of these will be a category heading. This might be things like 'skills', 'hobbies', and 'values'.

To determine the headings, look at your brainstorm and see what words could be grouped together. Then use your brainstorm to add words around each heading. For example, the heading might be 'skills' and the lines extending around the heading would describe your skills. These would be words like 'computer literate', 'time management' and so on.

Work through your brainstorm to sort the information on your mind map. Tick the words or draw a line through them as you go. Some words you won't use and that's fine. You don't have to use everything. By the end you should have an ordered picture that reflects who you are.

Your mind map will grow and develop as you do, so in the months and years ahead you can add to it. It's a good idea to update it at least once a year.

More Categories

I'm going to give you some more category headings, which I want you to explore. If you already have one or more of these on your sheet or something similar, go ahead and move on to the next one. Add these categories to your mind map and, as you do, see whether you have any information on your brainstorm you can add. If not, now is the time to think about some of these new categories and come up with additional points.

1. I am . . . (Complete this sentence in as many ways as you can) e.g. 'organized', 'punctual'

2. I want . . . (Complete this sentence in as many ways as you can)

3. I can . . . (Complete this sentence in as many ways as you can)

4. I know I'm good at. . .

5. I think I'm good at. . .

6. What's important to me in my personal life? (Personal values like honesty, love...)

7. What's important to me at work / in a job? (Work values like professional development...)

8. Qualifications

9. Education

10. Interests/Hobbies

11. What am I experienced at doing?

12. What skills do I have?

13. What can I do that others can't, don't or won't do?

14. What am I doing when I'm most engaged?

15. What have I done that's made a difference for others?

16. What are my achievements?

17. What are my top goals?

18. Words that describe my personality are . . .

19. What do others say I'm good at?

20. My ideal manager is. . .

21. My ideal work environment is. . .

22. If I didn't have to work for money, what would I do with my life?

23. My job expectations are. . .

24. The kind of people I like working with are . . .

25. What do I want people to say about me after I leave a job?

26. My strengths are . . .

27. How do I like success to be measured?

The 'So What?' Test

By this point, you'll have plenty of information on your mind map that's positive and affirms the value you have to offer. Now it's time to make sure you have both features *and* benefits listed.

For example, if you are by nature a team player that's a great feature but *so what?* What's the benefit of this to an employer? The benefit could be that you work well with others to achieve a common objective. How important is this benefit? It depends on the job. If you were part of a team designing a new motor vehicle, for instance, it would be hugely important.

Examine everything you've written down on your mind map and after each word or attribute ask, 'So what?' Wait for answers to come to mind. If they do, write them down. You see now why I often use larger sheets of paper.

Answers to the question 'So what?' will often come in the form of benefits. For example, if you'd written down that you possess great attention to detail and then asked *'So what?',* you may answer: I don't make many errors. I can work on my own. I don't need a lot of supervision. I'd make a great surgeon. Once you've established the stand out significance of your features, you will have an even clearer picture of the value you can offer to an employer.

The point of this chapter's exercises is to help you know yourself better than you ever have before. By now you should have no doubt that you have value to offer. It's a good idea to bring your mind map and other people's feedback out from time to time to remind yourself.

If you're not that happy with what you've learned about yourself, then this information is just as useful. What can you do differently to change how you and others see you? Be bold. Stand up and stand out whenever and wherever you get the chance. Next you're going to check that you actually believe that what you have to offer is of value and the complete solution to some employer's needs.

Chapter 5:

PERSPECTIVE CHECK

In this chapter, I'm going to help you check that you have the next piece in place — a winning perspective. This means believing and projecting that what you have to offer is the total solution to an employer's needs. If your perspective is not quite where it should be, I'll give you some practical tips to help you shift it into top gear.

What is Perspective?

How you view yourself, your world and the events in your life is called your perspective. Perspective is the window through which you view your world. This window often determines what happens next, and it can have a profound impact on what you experience. What you think, believe and say about yourself and how you project yourself, energizes and influences your desired outcomes.

As you go about your daily life, you're continually projecting your perspective, knowingly or not. You demonstrate this by what you think, say and do. It makes sense then to learn to become more aware of what your perspective is in relation to getting the job you want.

When you write your cover letter, you want to write it so it will represent what you believe about yourself. Writing a letter from a disempowered perspective will reflect in the outcome because it will not have the positive energy required to show your belief in yourself to the reader.

A Different Example

Let me give you a totally different example of how powerful a part your perspective can play in how things work or don't work out. Imagine seeing someone you find extremely attractive. You desperately want to connect with this person. If from your perspective, you don't believe you're quite 'in their league', then it's unlikely you'll be successful. Either you won't even try to talk to them or, when you do, it won't go anywhere fast. You won't feel confident, you won't expect success and you'll also project this to the other person.

Perhaps the person won't even notice you or, worse, they might reject you directly. You'll feel terrible and even less worthy. Your mind will tell you that this rejection proves you were right, which will unfortunately entrench this belief, especially if you repeat this kind of scenario often enough. Once it's a belief, it will become your default perspective. If you believe you're unworthy, you're setting yourself up for a self-fulling prophecy.

A Lesson from Hollywood

In *The Obstacle Is the Way*, author Ryan Holiday tells a story which perfectly illustrates how your perspective can impact your life. Apparently in the early days, George Clooney never got the parts he auditioned for. He wanted producers and directors to like him, but they didn't. The rejection hurt. He blamed them for not seeing how amazing an actor he was.

Today he's a well-known, high profile actor. What changed? Once he became aware of his self-limiting perspective, he changed it. And when he changed how he viewed himself, everything changed. Up to that point he had believed he needed to be 'selected', that getting a part was controlled completely by the producers and directors. From his perspective, he was an unemployed actor with a problem. All the power, he had thought, was with others.

Then he realized that the producers also had a problem—they needed to find an actor as much as he needed to act. They were hoping the next person to audition would be that special person, that perfect actor. Auditions were a chance for *them* to solve *their* problem, not for him to solve his problem. With this new mindset he no longer projected that he was desperate to be chosen. Rather he believed and conveyed that he was someone with something special to offer. He was the solution to their problem, not the other way around.

What About You?

To get the job you want, you also need to operate from a winning perspective. When you apply for a job do you expect to succeed? Do you know without any doubt that you're the solution they're looking for? If you do, then you'll believe it's the perfect job for you, that you're the best person for it, that you have everything they're looking for and that the job is as good as yours.

But if there's even a hint of self-doubt in your perspective, you'll project a completely different attitude. You'll feel unsure. You'll hope it works out, but maybe it won't. You'll really want them to like and choose you. If only they'd give you a chance, you could show them that you can do it.

A Salesperson's Perspective

As you now know, you need to sell yourself when you apply for a job—you need to be a salesperson. The most successful sales people have no doubt their product is of immense value to a prospective customer. They believe that what they have to offer is the perfect solution.

You too have to operate from the perspective of a confident salesperson, solving the needs of a customer by offering them the very best 'product' to do the job—you. Believe in yourself. Know without a doubt your services will completely fulfil their needs. From this and only from this perspective will you be successful.

An employer has requirements. You can meet them or not, but your employer needs to believe you can meet them before they'll hire you. For them to believe, you have to believe and you need to project that belief on your face, in your body language and in the cover letter you're going to write.

That's one of the reasons I had you brainstorm everything that makes you valuable, to give you a basis for your new perspective. Everything you are and have become to date is what you can offer an employer. These are your personal employment assets—your features and benefits. The more relevant and extensive your assets are, the more in demand you'll be. So you came up with the hard evidence of why you stand out, but it has to go beyond pen and paper, you have to believe it and live it too.

Checking Your Perspective

So how do you know what kind of perspective you're operating from? The way you feel about it will give you the biggest clue. When you think about a job you want how do you feel? Do you feel light, confident, certain, excited and good about it or do you feel anxious, doubtful and fearful? Positive feelings mean that you are operating from a positive perspective. Negative feelings mean your perspective is negative.

Another clue to your perspective is how you talk to others about a job. Do you tell everybody you see that you've applied and how excited you are about it? Or do you tell nobody? If you tell no one, why is that? Maybe you don't believe you stand a chance. Maybe you don't want to explain that you failed when you fail, so you keep your application to yourself. All this does is entrench a negative perspective.

Even if you do speak to others about the job, how positive is your language and attitude? Saying something like, 'This is the perfect job for me, and I know I'll be great doing what they require.' is very different from 'I'm not really sure it's for me, but if it's meant to be then I guess it will work out.'

To figure out your current perspective, note how you feel and what you're thinking and saying about the situation.

How to Shift Your Perspective

Once you're aware of your perspective, you can shift it if required. You have a choice about how you view life—positively or negatively. Changing your perspective is nothing more than changing the window through which you view the situation. When you make a decision to change how you view the world, you change how you feel about it, which in turn changes how you think and act.

Try the following to help you think and act from a different perspective:

1. Acknowledge that you choose your perspective and that you can shift it when you choose to do so.

2. Look at the self-assessment work you did in the previous chapter. Remind yourself why you are the best person for the job. You have the hard evidence in front of you.

3. Express and enact a perspective that will serve you. Tell people that you're applying for an amazing job. Get excited when you speak to them about it and why you are perfect for it. Don't even entertain the notion that you might not be successful. When you articulate and enact a desired perspective, you reinforce it and signal to others that you believe it too.

4. Surround yourself with people who support,

encourage and believe in you. They will also affirm that you will be successful, helping build positive momentum.

5. If you have any doubts, look for a role model, someone who has the attitude you want to have, and ask how they would behave were they in the same situation. Refer back to how George Clooney changed his perspective in order to be successful.

6. Imagine already doing the job. Casually daydream or use a more structured visualization technique. Make sure when you visualize that you use as many of your senses as possible, in particular focus on how great you're feeling while you're in your dream job.

7. Self-talk and affirmations can also be a powerful tool for positive focus. An affirmation is a statement that you repeat to help program your mind to be positive. Some examples, 'I'm the perfect candidate for this job', 'If anybody can, I can.', 'This is the best job ever for me.'

In this chapter, you took the next step in preparing to write your cover letter. It's not enough to theoretically know why you stand out; you must believe and live it too. Approach each job application certain that you are the best person to do the job. Decide to be free of self-doubt. Train yourself to only expect success. When you do, this attitude will also come across in your sales letter. Now, it's time to make sure the jobs you're applying for are the best for you and that you are quite clear about what they are looking for.

Chapter 6:

IS IT THE RIGHT JOB?

You now have a clear picture of who you are and what you have to offer. You also know how important it is to operate from the right perspective, one that gives you the very best chance of succeeding. Time to find out more about the job you want to apply for. You need to be sure it aligns with what's important to you, matches what you have to offer and, just as importantly, fits your career objectives.

There's no short cut to deciding whether a job is right for you. You're going to have to ask and answer a lot of questions. For your convenience I have also reproduced these in the downloadable workbook. You can complete this exercise using a specific job advertisement or more generally if you are only thinking about whether a type of job might suit you.

If the job you're applying for is unfamiliar, but lacking in specifics, you'll need to do some research. Working through these questions will help you know what you still need to find out. Research can be done using the Internet or by calling the company and asking for more information such as a detailed job description.

Sadly, many people end up in jobs they don't love. This is often purely because they need to pay bills and someone has agreed to hire them. This route is a sure recipe for unhappiness. Your life will feel consumed by 'work' rather than filled with the joy of doing something you love.

If you believe you can't do what you want to do, you'll settle for second best. A stand out approach is different however. Decide what you really want to do and believe you can do it. Then find a way to make it happen. If it's important enough, you will. Just remember not to be completely unrealistic when it comes how much time it may take to get there. Depending on your circumstances, you may have to work your way to your dream job in a few steps, but if it's the right job for you and it's that important why wouldn't you do this?

A warning about the questions that follow: there are a lot of them. Answering all sixty every time you apply for a job would be extremely arduous and also unnecessary. I suggest you answer as many as you need to get a good idea of whether the job is suitable for you. Some may not be relevant to the job you're reviewing. Leave them out. Also not all of them require a written response. You only need to write responses to those that could be helpful for your letter and resume.

1. What are the main tasks that will be required?
2. What problems/needs does this role fulfil in their organization?
3. What problems/needs will result if they don't have someone in this role?

4. What problems/needs will result if they have someone in this role who is not the right person or who doesn't do the job as required?

5. How does this job fit into what I have been doing most recently for work?

6. What future career options could be available to me later if I were to take this job?

7. Where is this job located? Is it feasible for me to make this commute twice a day every day?

8. What hours is the job likely to demand?

9. What salary and other conditions are offered?

10. Is overtime involved? How much? Is it paid above the job's salary?

11. Is travel involved? How much?

12. What kind of work environment is involved? (E.g. office, factory, outdoors, construction site.)

13. Are there any unusual conditions under which I will have to perform? (Weather, isolation, security, etc.)

14. What, if any, special qualifications are required?

15. Is any special training required? Do I have it? If not, do they offer to pay for it, or must I do this before or after starting the job?

16. Is a particular talent required? Do I have this? Can it be learned?

17. What skills are required? (Social/interpersonal, mathematical, spatial, artistic, manual, dexterity, communication, technological, etc.)

18. Is the job dangerous? In what way?

19. What are the health risks?

20. Is there a high learning expectation over the course of this job, with constant change involved? If so would I like this or would it be too stressful? Be realistic, you must know your limits.

21. Is this a routine job, with very little change involved? Would I like this or would it be boring?

22. What kind of interaction with the public is expected? High or low public contact?

23. What do people love about this job? What do they dislike about it?

24. Is physical appearance an important element in determining employment in this type of work?

25. What physical requirements define who is accepted into this line of work? (Vision, height, weight restrictions, and flexibility are common requirements.)

26. What part does honesty, integrity, or a code of ethics play in the performance of this work?

27. Will I need to be part of an organization, a particular religion, or a certain political persuasion to be considered for this job?

28. How important is natural charisma and persuasive ability in doing well in this job?

29. Do I have any disabilities? How can I make this work for me rather than against me?

30. What are my most important or strongest needs right now?

31. What questions, unique to my life and situation, do I need to have answered? Write them down.

32. Do I feel that this work is worthwhile for me?

33. Will this work affect my home life? Put stress on my family? Strain my relationship?

34. Will I have time for my own personal leisure activities, interests and hobbies?

35. Can I see myself doing this work and being happy at it? Why? Why not?

36. What kind of a contribution will I be making to my community through this work? Is this important to me? Why?

37. Will this job require me to make major changes to my lifestyle? What are they? Am I comfortable with this?

38. Does this work fit my personality type? What is my personality type?

39. Will my central motivations keep me interested in this kind of work?

40. Can I use my preferred intelligences in this job?

41. Does this job satisfy my work preferences? (Realistic, investigative, artistic, social, enterprising or conventional and so on.)

42. How do I find out more about this job?

43. If I was this employer, who would my ideal candidate be?

44. What problems would I be solving in this job?

45. What would be the worst kind of person for this employer to take on?

46. What would the company expect of me?

47. Why have they advertised this job?

48. Is there anything about this job that concerns me?

49. What would be the best part of this job?

50. What would the worst part be of this job?

51. What direct experience do I have for this job?

52. What indirect (transferrable) experience/skills do I have for this job?

53. What does this employer/company value?

54. Make a list of everything they are looking for. (Qualities, experience, values, etc.)

55. What achievements would they value?

56. Does this job fit in with my current and future career goals?

57. Would I love doing this job every day? Why? Why not?

58. If money wasn't an issue, would I do this job for no pay?

59. Am I still interested in this job?

60. What is the name of the person to whom I must address my letter?

By the time you've worked through enough of the above questions, you should also have an idea of whether what you can offer aligns with what they require. If it's a good match, you're ready to learn how to put this all together by writing your new cover letter or as we're now calling it, your sales letter.

Chapter 7:

HOW TO WRITE YOUR SALES LETTER

The sales letter format I'm going to teach you follows the classic marketing mantra - 'create a problem, be the solution.' Even though there's only one letter format, I'll cover three slightly different variations. The one you use will depend on whether you're applying to an advertisement, approaching a company without knowing if they have a job (otherwise known as cold prospecting) or using a referral. I'm going to cover all three in this chapter.

The Invited Letter

You send an invited letter when you're applying for a job in response to an advertisement. This letter will always be tailored primarily to the job requirements detailed in the advertisement. For our purposes I'm going to apply to the following fictional job advertisement:

NEW AUTO SALESPERSON

Do you want to work in a modern, indoor showroom with great people for the biggest ABC dealership in Blueton?

We currently have an exciting opportunity for an experienced sales person to join our dynamic New Car Sales team at our Blueton dealership. We pride ourselves on delivering the best service to every customer, every time! Want to work for the most reputable and professional car dealership in Blueton?

We offer extensive staff training and an exciting working environment. This rare opportunity includes:

- Continuous training and development courses
- Indoor, air-conditioned showrooms
- Fantastic earning potential—generous base salary + commissions + company vehicle

Are you looking for a change or new challenge? Are you a people person who has:

- A desire to achieve results.
- A strong work ethic and sales flare.
- Exceptional customer service skills.
- A willingness to work weekends (we are flexible on this).

Regardless of your specific experience, if you have a proven track record in sales or delivering exceptional customer service this could be the position for you! We are willing to train the right person with the right attitude.

To be considered for this position you must have a current and valid driver's licence, professional communication skills and outstanding customer service skills. As a New Vehicle Sales Executive your day will consist of gaining business from new and existing customers, interpreting buying criteria and decision making processes whilst maintaining in-depth knowledge of our vehicles and products.

Join Blueton ABC and become part of our high performing sales team! If this is the position you have been looking for, put your career into drive and apply now via the link below.

Due to the high volume of applications expected, only short-listed candidates will be contacted.

What is the Blueton Auto Dealership Looking For?

All commercial companies are in business to make money, so the auto dealership is looking for staff to help them achieve this. Staff could make the business money by generating sales directly or indirectly by saving them money, time, or contributing skills and experience that can be used to grow the company.

In the summary below I have listed the features ABC Blueton are looking for and, in parenthesis, I have indicated how having someone as described will benefit them.

- Experience not necessarily in the motor industry but in customer service/sales, proven track record in sales or customer service, right attitude. (The benefit of employing someone who fulfils this requirement is that the company will save time on training and coaching, which means such a person can start generating sales quickly)

- Results driven. (Someone who is results driven will achieve targets and that means increased sales.)

- Strong work ethic (Someone who has a strong work ethic won't be lazy. They will do the job and meet expectations, which will help increase sales.)

- Flare for sales. (Someone who is naturally sales-oriented will require less supervision, saving time and hopefully leading to more sales.)

- Exceptional customer service skills. (Happy customers are return customers and that means increased sales)

- Willing to work weekends. (Having someone work at their busiest times means maximizing the potential of a good salesperson, which will increase sales)

- Current and valid driver's license. (An auto salesperson who drives, especially the company's vehicles, will be a good representative, which could increase sales.)

- Professional communication skills. (The better someone can communicate, the better chances they will have of closing deals, which means increased sales)

- Can gain business from new and existing customers. (Finding business means making more sales.)

- Can interpret the buying and decision-making processes (Having this skill means someone will be able to close more deals.)
- In-depth knowledge of vehicles and products. (Knowing the product they're selling will help them to be a better salesperson and make more money.)

The Eight Sales Letter Writing Steps

Your letter should follow a professional business format, observing any specific letter-writing requirements in your part of the world. It should, at the very least, contain your address, the date written and be addressed by name to the person. I also suggest that you include the title of the role you're applying for at the top of your letter.

Each of the eight steps will be explained followed by a portion of a sample letter in reply to the auto dealership job.

Step 1 - State the problem

Your opening paragraph must outline the problem that the job you're applying for will solve. Think about the problem the company might have if the job isn't filled or if it was to be filled by the wrong person.

Let's look at an example:

If someone was looking to employ a car salesperson, what problems might they be encountering that this role would solve?

Keeping it simple, they may not have someone to service their existing customers so they're losing sales.

They might also not have someone who can bring in new business so they're losing sales to competitors.

This is a traditional and time tested copywriting technique that writers of sales letters have used to great effect—present a problem, then solve it. (Which we'll do in step two.)

In other words, what need or problem does this role help solve? You want the reader to identify with this problem. Even if a recruiter is going to read it first, ultimately your aim is to get your letter in front of the hiring manager so write to the person who will employ you.

State the problem boldly and bluntly. Keep it short and to the point. A one sentence paragraph is fine here if that's all it takes.

'In today's competitive new auto sales market, if you don't have an extraordinary sales team in place, you'll experience falling sales, failed targets and a declining business.'

I've written this so the hiring manager can relate to the problem at a personal level, since he or she will ultimately be responsible for the team's sales.

Step 2 - Present the solution

Next you're going to announce that you're the solution to the problem. What you're saying to the reader is, that if you'll continue reading, I'll show how I'm the solution to the problem I've just described above.

'Finding the right person who fits in with your team, is able to service existing needs and increase business is not always easy to find. Allow me to demonstrate why I believe I'm someone who can contribute to your team's future successes.'

Once again I'm appealing directly to the hiring manager's need to succeed and pointing out that I can help make this happen.

Step 3 - Establish your credibility

You've presented the problem and offered yourself as the solution. Now you must show why you are a credible or trustworthy option for them to consider. What will make them want to read further? The easiest way to establish this is by telling them how your past experience is relevant.

If your skills and experience are indirectly relevant, you need to explain how. For example, you may have sales skills but not in this particular industry. For this job, that wouldn't be a problem, because the advertisement makes it quite clear that they are willing to train someone with the right attitude. Here's where you would demonstrate that right attitude.

Or, if you have little professional experience in this field, refer to other applicable experiences. For example, if the role required experience in managing people, but you had only had one short job in management, you could mention that you managed a club at college or that you captained a sports team for many years.

This part of the letter builds more rapport with the reader as you prove that you're a candidate they should take seriously. Questions you want to answer here: What experience did they state they were looking for in the advertisement? How do you meet this?

'With over six years' sales experience, three of which have been working for a competitor auto dealership, I'm well acquainted with what's required to do this job.'

Step 4 - Demonstrate the benefits of employing you

In this part of the letter you spell out how you fulfil their needs and how this will benefit their business. Don't cover everything they mention in the advertisement. Choose two or three traits you're confident about which you think they'll find important.

The words, 'this means' is a useful way to link features and benefits. Make sure you use some of the main keywords from their advertisement. These will also likely be words that an ATS system will search for. Write these as bullet points and bold type the keywords to get their attention and help them read through. Remember to test each feature with the 'So what? question to find an accompanying benefit.

- *I have a strong **desire to achieve results,** which means I am driven to achieve and exceed all personal sales targets.*

- *My **exceptional customer service skills** mean my clients tend to become repeat customers who refer me to their personal networks, generating an endless chain of prospects from whom I gain ongoing business.*

Step 5 – Prove that you're an above average achiever

Employers are not interested to know that you carried out just the necessary tasks. They expect that. What they want to know is how you made a difference personally or to the company as a whole. In other words, here you'll highlight achievements that made a difference to past employers which will likely predict future success should these new employers hire you.

Once again, include no more than two to three of your most relevant achievements. Employers like achievements that contribute to a financial bottom line with a quantified result. Most bottom lines can be measured. Aim to express this as increases in sales, decreases in costs, increases in market share and other changes to an organization's key performance indicators. Percentages or fractions work particularly well here. So think numbers and measures.

It's best to express this in a particular way—what you did, how you did it and what happened as a result. What you want to demonstrate is tangible and related proof. By the way, generally employers do not regard an award as an achievement. This is about what you achieved beyond expectations. What extraordinary difference did you make? In other words, how did you stand out? Test every achievement by asking 'So what?'

*'You may be interested to know that in my previous role I sourced and implemented new customer relationship management software which **reduced** the number of calls the service centre received **by 25%** over the first 12 months. This meant we could redeploy six staff to the field thereby **increasing our market share** by a further 4%. I also attained **300%** of my **sales targets** in 2013, **600%** in 2014, and **725%** in 2015. This contributed to growing the branch **market share by 6%** over three years.'*

Step 6 - Make them a promise

Now you want to make them a promise that's bold and enticing but doesn't create a problem for you further down the line. The last thing you want to do is make promises you're not sure you can keep. For example, you don't want to say you'll increase their sales by a certain percentage. How do you know you can? Remember you have no idea what you're actually getting yourself into until you're there. You may well find factors beyond your control prevent you from fulfilling your promise.

Rather the promise you make must be attached to your number one work value, which should illustrate your work ethic and philosophy. It must define your attitude more than anything else. If you're stuck for this go back to your self-assessment answers and see what you wrote down in response to the question "What's important to me at work/in a job?"

In particular look for things you wrote down that are centred around other people. Choose the one that's most important to you and which will be important to them. One piece of advice: don't make promises you know you can't keep or that you don't believe in one hundred percent. If you can't make a genuine promise, leave this step out. If you can make a promise I suggest starting this part with 'I believe . . .'

'I believe in contributing, learning and growing as an employee wherever I work, and I promise that this will be my top priority when I work for you.'

Take note, not *'if I work for you'* but *'**when** I work for you.'*

Step 7 - Warn them you're on the market

Regardless of whether you're actively applying for jobs elsewhere or not, you must always create the impression you are. Creating time sensitivity and scarcity are common sales strategies. They work because nobody wants to feel like they're going to miss out on a great opportunity and then regret it later. Take care not to sound too sure of yourself, or even arrogant. I advise you start this step with where they can find out more about you.

'For more detail about my work history, achievements and qualifications, please see my resume. I realise you probably have many applications to consider and a process to follow, but I'd also like you to know that I'm actively marketing myself right now so I can finalize my next career move as soon as possible.'

Step 8 - Call to action

Now encourage them to move you to the next step in their process. You'll also show that you'll be following up with them. This demonstrates that you're an action taker who's serious about the job. Why would anyone not want to employ someone like you?

'Finally, it would be my pleasure to meet with you to discuss this role further. Please note, since this opportunity is important to me I will be following up in a few days to see where we are in the process.'

So finally this is what the letter looks like -

Dear Jack Smith,

New Auto Salesperson

In today's competitive new auto sales market, if you don't have an extraordinary sales team in place, you'll experience falling sales, failed targets and a declining business. Finding the right person who fits in with your team, is able to service existing needs and increase business is not always easy to find. Allow me to demonstrate why I believe I'm someone who can contribute to your team's future successes.

With over six years' sales experience, three of which have been working for a competitor auto dealership, I'm well acquainted with what's required to do this job.

- I have a strong **desire to achieve results,** which means I am driven to achieve and exceed all personal sales targets.

- My **exceptional customer service skills** mean my clients tend to become repeat customers who refer me to their personal networks, generating an endless chain of prospects from whom I gain ongoing business.

You may be interested to know that in my previous role I sourced and implemented new customer relationship management software which **reduced** the number of calls the service centre received **by 25%** over the first 12 months. This meant we could redeploy six staff to the field thereby **increasing our market share** by a further 4%. I also attained **300%** of my **sales targets** in 2013, **600%** in 2014, and **725%** in 2015. This contributed to growing the branch **market share by 6%** over three years.

I believe in contributing, learning and growing as an employee wherever I work, and I promise that this will be my top priority when I work for you.

For more detail about my work history, achievements and qualifications, please see my resume. I realise you probably have many applications to consider and a process to follow, but I'd also like you to know that I'm actively marketing myself right now so I can finalize my next career move as soon as possible.

Finally, it would be my pleasure to meet with you to discuss this role further. Please note, since this opportunity is important to me I will be following up in a few days to see where we are in the process.

Yours faithfully,
Tom Brown

The Uninvited Letter

Did you know it's said that only 20% of jobs are ever publically advertised? If you only apply for that 20%, you could be missing out on the other 80% of hidden jobs, not yet and perhaps never to be advertised.

Writing an uninvited letter involves researching to find jobs you'd like to undertake at companies of your choosing and then writing to them to offer your services. This is also called a cold-contact sales letter. It is, by far, the best way to tap into the hidden job market.

There's a greater chance your sales letter and application will be read by one of these companies since most job seekers don't use this approach. This means they will often receive your application when they are not being swamped by others. Companies are also understandably usually curious about job seekers who are this proactive. Even with no vacancies, they will often offer to keep your application on file for a period of time in case any suitable roles come up.

The way in which you should approach this letter is not too different from the invited letter. Below I'll explain where you should make some changes.

Step 1 – State the problem

As long as the company you approach has a need for the type of job you're interested in, you can write about the problem as if they have a vacancy. There could be one, after all. In short, just write this section like the default letter.

Step 2 - Present the solution

This will remain the same, except for the last part of the second sentence.

'Finding the right person who fits in with your team, is able to service existing needs and increase business is not always easy to find. Allow me to demonstrate why I believe I'm someone who can contribute to your team's future successes should you have a current vacancy or should a vacancy come up soon.'

Step 3 - Establish your Credibility

No changes here.

Step 4 - Demonstrate the Benefits of employing you

The features that a company looks for are generally similar. You can always look at jobs that are being advertised for similar roles and choose their features as a guide.

Step 5 - Prove that you're an above average achiever

No changes here. Just relate these to the job for which you're applying.

Step 6 - Make them a promise

No changes here.

Step 7 - Warn them that you're on the market

You do need to modify this part to acknowledge that you're cold prospecting and that you'd like to be considered now or in the future.

'For more detail about my work history, achievements and qualifications please see my resume. I realise you may not have any current vacancies, but I'd like you to know that I'm actively marketing myself at this stage. If you do have vacancies now or in the future, I'd very much like to be considered as an applicant.'

Step 8 - Call to action

The ending requires changes to make for an appropriate conclusion.

'It would be my pleasure to meet with you now or in the future to discuss any suitable vacancies. Please note that because I have especially earmarked yours as company of choice I will be following up within a few days to ascertain whether an opportunity exists at this stage.'

The Referral Letter

The third job application sales letter uses name-dropping to get an employer's attention and is another excellent way to tap into the hidden job market.

In the world of sales, no marketing tool is more valuable than word-of-mouth. The referral letter is based on this idea. When a mutual acquaintance tips you off to job or a company, they are, in effect, recommending you. Using his or her name to your advantage in a sales letter can have a dramatic impact. Make sure to ask permission to use their name.

The referral letter could be for a current vacancy or it could be a cold-prospecting letter. Follow the invited or uninvited approach based on the situation.

The change to this letter comes right at the start. It's

an extra step that drops the name of the person who referred you before you move into the remainder of your letter.

Dear Jack Smith,

A mutual acquaintance of ours, Tom Billings, *suggested I write to you about the current vacancy you have for a new auto salesperson.*

In today's competitive new auto sales market, if you don't have an extraordinary sales team in place, you may experience falling sales, failed targets and declining business.

OR

Dear Jack Smith,

A mutual acquaintance of ours, Tom Billings, *suggested I write to you about any vacancies you may have for a new auto salesperson, either currently or in the not too distant future.*

In today's competitive new auto sales market, if you don't have an extraordinary team in place, you may experience falling sales, failed targets and declining business.

In this chapter I have shown you step by step how to construct your sales letter, whether it's invited, uninvited or a referral. The steps are as follows:

Step 1 - State the problem

Step 2 - Present the solution

Step 3 - Establish your credibility

Step 4 - Demonstrate the benefits of employing you

Step 5 - Prove that you're an above average achiever

Step 6 - Make them a promise

Step 7 - Warn them you're on the market

Step 8 - Call to action

You now know how to write your sales letter. With practice you will get better at writing these letters. In the next chapter I've provided more examples of sales letters that follow this format.

Chapter 8:

MORE LETTER EXAMPLES

In this chapter I've included three more sample letters. Each of these is different and covers one of the three types of letters—invited, uninvited and referral. As you read them, see if you can identify how I've integrated the eight steps covered in the previous chapter. I included these letters to demonstrate that this format can work no matter the industry and level of job you're applying for.

Example 1 – An Invited letter for an accounts / admin assistant role

Job Advertisement

Accounts/Admin Assistant - Full Time

LivingLife is an iconic bohemian brand, celebrating freedom of expression and creativity. We currently have 28 stores nationwide and believe our tribe is the key to our success. We are seeking a fun, vibrant office all-rounder to join our Head Office team and be part of creating the best bohemian shopping experience.

Responsibilities of this position will include

- Answer telephone enquiries, screen and transfer inbound phone calls
- Daily bank reconciliations for all stores and variance follow up
- Maintain electronic and hardcopy filing system
- Data entry
- Maintenance of freight costing spreadsheet and invoice posting
- Open, sort and distribute incoming mail
- Maintain staff visa statements records, travelling expenses and petty cash expenditure
- General office duties

Experience

- Computer skills – intermediate Microsoft Excel
- Knowledge of clerical and administrative procedures
- 1-2 years' experience in a similar role

Key Competencies

- Good communication skills – written and verbal
- Planning and organizing
- Prioritizing
- Attention to detail and accuracy
- Ability to work as part of a team

- Customer service orientation

If you are looking for a unique, inspiring and positive place to work, apply to Sally Clifford now to join the LivingLife team. Only applicants who meet the above requirements will be considered.

Sales Letter

Dear Sally Clifford,

Accounts / Admin Assistant

Without efficient, organized and accurate admin support, the daily running of an office can soon turn into a nightmare. Imagine if inbound calls are not effectively screened, someone forgets to follow up on identified variances or claims they're Excel proficient and then requires constant tutoring in order to complete freight costing and invoice mailing.

Having these skills is something that has always come naturally to me which is why I moved into this role as a career two years ago.

- I am adept at **planning and organizing,** which means you'll enjoy the benefits of day to day order and clarity, saving you and your staff time when it matters most.

- I regard **detail and accuracy** as critical in my own life, which means I'll get the job done with no or little supervision so you can attend to more important matters.

*Working at XYZ Company, I **introduced a new user friendly in-store filing system** which **reduced** file retrieval time by **30%,** assisting staff to **increase** their face-to-face time with customers. I also **designed and introduced*** *my own phone call screening template, which helped me* **resolve** *the majority of incoming product enquiries. This led to a* **reduction** *in transferring incoming contacts by up to* **25%** *on a daily basis.*

I love what I do so I view my job as more than just a job. As a result, I can promise you that I will give 100% to my work when you employ me as part of your team.

Please note, I am currently actively looking for alternative employment. This role at your company is at the top of my shortlist; however, I have also applied for other positions as I want to finalize my next career move as soon as possible.

To find out more about me please see my resume. It would also be wonderful to meet with you to discuss how I can add further value to your organization. Since this opportunity is important to me, I will be following up in a few days to see where we are at in the process.

Yours faithfully,
Heather Jackson

Example 2 – An uninvited sales letter written to enquire whether a company has a need for a social media/marketing specialist

Dear Scott Banks,

Social Media/Marketing Specialist

In today's fast changing digital space, any company not effectively exploiting all aspects of the social medial marketing map is missing out on key customer engagement and website traffic opportunities, potentially resulting in thousands of dollars in lost revenue.

Do you require a Social Media/Marketing specialist to assist your business? I have run a successful part-time online business of my own for the last three years, where I have implemented effective social media campaigns as my principle marketing channel. Most of my formal work experience, however, has been as a hospitality trainer where I also used social media marketing strategies to recruit new students.

- *I currently* **generate, edit, publish and share daily content** *(photo/video/text), which means I'll be able to do the same for your company, building meaningful connections and encouraging your target audience to take action on offers presented.*

- *I am* **detail and customer oriented** *with good multitasking and organizational abilities, which means I'm able to monitor customer satisfaction accurately as part of a system workflow while focusing on all major marketing channels simultaneously.*

Over the last 12 months I have **grown** *my business email database to over* **20 000** *subscribers, which means I have a strong and growing list I can market to at any time. This has* **increased my monthly income by 14%.** *I've also built a* **Facebook** *page with over* **70,000 fans and have a Twitter following of 18,000.** *This has assisted me to capture relevant social data / metrics, insights and best practice, allowing me to act on information instantly.*

I believe in rising to challenges and making a difference using social media, which I promise is what I will be committed to achieving should you currently have a role for me in your organization.

Please see my resume for additional work history, achievements and qualifications. I realise you may not have any current vacancies, but should one arise in the not too distant future, please keep me in mind. I am actively marketing myself at this stage in order to finalize my next career move as soon as possible.

It would be my pleasure to meet with you to discuss any possible roles available. Please note, that because I have earmarked your company for this enquiry, I will be following up within a few days to ascertain whether a current opportunity exists or not.

Yours faithfully,
Jane Abbott

Example 3 – A referral sales letter written to secure an operations manager role for a food production company

Dear Matthew Willis,

Operations Manager

I recently met your IT Manager, Nick Small, who was telling me about your company's plans for expansion and that you may be looking to employ a new Operations Manager. Considering your circumstances, engaging anybody who is unable to wear multiple hats will severely impact the smooth running of your company, especially in the areas of delivery management, daily operations as well as supply chain and inventory management.

If you're seeking a multitasking personality to be your next Operations Manager, then look no further. Having been in a similar role at Fuel Source for the last 8 years and in similar roles previous to this, I have extensive experience across multiple operational disciplines.

- *I possess strong **leadership** qualities having **managed over 60 employees and 20 suppliers** in my current role. This means I am ideally positioned to assist* *you with **developing operations** across the country.*

- *I can also work with **embedding processes and systems** as required. This means I'll be able to ensure the smooth running of cost-efficient production processes and the timely delivery of product to new warehouse sites.*

*In 2015, I attained an **18% reduction** in operating costs by auditing and simplifying contractor processes, which ultimately increased the company's bottom line profits. I also introduced an appropriate IT system to manage forecasting, order placement and fulfilment including performance evaluation, which resulted in greater accuracy and a **25% reduction** in unnecessary wastage.*

I am committed to being a dynamic leader and promise to lead and inspire your people while developing and growing your business.

Please see my resume for additional work history, achievements and qualifications. I realise you may well have others to consider and a process to follow, but I'd like you to know that I'm actively marketing myself at this stage in order to finalize my next career move as soon as possible.

It would be my pleasure to meet with you so we can both assess whether we are a right fit for each other. Please note, because this opportunity is important to me I will be following up within a few days to assess where we are at in the process.

Yours faithfully,
Tom Brown

In this chapter I have provided you with three further examples that follow the sales letter format. The exact wording in the letters is not as important as following the format provided. In the next chapter, I'll touch on what you can to do to ensure you get past the dreaded ATS software.

Chapter 9:

MAKING YOUR LETTER
ATS COMPLIANT

Applicant Tracking System (ATS) software is used by an increasing number of employers and recruitment agencies today to assist them with handling their recruitment needs. According to job search services provider Preptel, this same software is responsible for rejecting as many as 75% of job applications. In this chapter, I'm going to tell you exactly how this application reading robot works and what you can do to ensure that your letter and resume are compliant.

Does ATS Apply to Cover Letters or Just Resumes?

Not all ATS software is capable of or programmed to read cover letters, but since you don't know for sure, why take a chance? Today, a well-crafted cover letter and resume must also be ATS friendly. To increase your chances of having your letter read, I suggest that, unless otherwise requested, always keep your letter and resume as one document so they're less likely to be separated. ATS software can't usually tell how long a document is; it searches purely for relevant keywords. Although I will refer to your letter in this chapter, this information applies to your resume as well.

How Does It Work?

Without getting too technical, the software searches for information in your application, which it then places in specific fields inside its database. This could be work experience, education, contact information or any number of things. Then it analyses the data for criteria relevant to the position being offered. After analysing the data, it assigns a score to each application, ranking the candidates against each other so that the best applications can be selected for human eyes.

How can you make sure that your letter gets past the filter and possibly bumped up to the top?

How to Make Your Letter Compliant

1. Make sure that the ATS can read your letter. Keep your fonts and formatting simple. Often this type of software will scan your file and convert information to a text format and then extract the relevant information from there. Creative layouts and graphics will not work in your favour.

2. Preferably use a text format like .doc or .docx. Some ATS software can't read PDF documents, so don't risk it. Definitely don't scan your application as an image as images won't be processed at all.

72

3. Don't use tables and columns and no WordArt. Also, don't interfere with character spacing.

4. Use the date format relevant to the country you're applying in and make sure you include dates in full—day, month and year—to make them easily identifiable.

5. Stick with standard industry words. For instance, don't use the word 'abilities' in place of 'skills' because you hope it might get more attention. Remember this is software that has been programmed to search for standard terms. Use standard words like 'work experience', 'skills' and 'education' so that you don't run the risk of your information being misread or being placed in the wrong categories.

6. You must include targeted keywords that are pertinent to your industry and the actual job. You will find these used in the job advertisement as well as the position description. The latter is not always available but you can request this from the company.

7. Don't 'stuff' your letter with too many keywords. Some ATS software penalizes applications for having lists of too many keywords in their documents. Select the most relevant for the position you're applying for. Also if yours does come up for human review, it will be discarded if the reader believes you were trying to 'work the system'.

8. Use 'buzzwords' that are currently being used for the job and industry you're in. This could be words like, 'coordinate', 'manage', 'project manage', 'team leader' or so on.

9. Include industry jargon and abbreviations if this is pertinent. Make sure you always spell out the abbreviations.

10. Ensure you focus on key areas such as skills, education, years of experience and names of former employers, which are common to all ATS searches.

Now, for some common cover letter mistakes to avoid:

Chapter 10:

COVER LETTER MISTAKES TO AVOID

As you write your own letters, you'll make your own mistakes and, hopefully, learn from them. But you should also learn from others' mistakes. In this chapter, I'm including the most common mistakes people make when writing cover letters or, as you now call them, sales letters. Follow the format I've taught you and avoid the following mistakes at all costs.

Separating Your Resume from Your Sales Letter

Unless the site asks you to upload these documents separately, always, always, always keep them as one document. When you package these as one, you'll have a far better chance of them staying together when they're read and passed on to other parties.

Not Including Your Letter as Text in Your Email

If you're sending your application via email, copy your sales letter to the body of your e-mail as well as including it with your resume. This way you'll have twice the chance of someone reading your sales letter.

Using the Wrong Letter Tone

In other words, don't write a letter as you would to a friend. A sales letter is a business document that must be professional in every sense. Avoid abbreviations, especially texting abbreviations. Use a standard business-letter format. It should include the date, the recipient's mailing address and your return address.

Ignoring the Company's Needs

Your letter should be about the employer as much as about you. You do need to tell the employer about yourself, but do so in the context of the employer's needs and the specified job requirements. The focus must be on how you meet the company's needs. This letter isn't a forum for sharing your life story or explaining why you're so great. Instead, show them how you being great will help them.

Making Unsupported Claims

Your claims must be backed up with evidence. Without this, you're just making an empty boast. Employers need proof. Remember too that your sales letter is itself evidence of your written communication skills. Too often I've seen someone say they possess 'excellent written communication skills' when their sales letter is proof of the opposite.

Writing Letters That Are Generic, Say Nothing or Which Duplicate Your Resume

Don't send generic cover letters or, in other words, the exact same letter for all applications. Jobs might be similar but companies never are. Tailor your letter specifically to the advertisement.

Also don't write cover letters that say absolutely nothing, since these add nothing to your application. Don't just copy and paste huge chunks of your resume to your letter. What's the point of saying the same thing twice?

Sounding Desperate

Do not beg them to consider you and do not explain how you have to get this job or you will starve to death. Nothing turns others off more than desperation.

Copying and Pasting Letters from the Internet

You want your letter to be original and authentic. You can only represent your letter in person if you have written a genuine letter from the heart.

Addressing Your Letters Impersonally

Personalized greetings carry a lot of power. People like to feel they're important, and nothing makes a person feel more important than hearing/reading their own name. If the name isn't supplied in the advertisement, you should call the company to find out what it is.

Telling the Employer What the Company Can Do for You

This mistake is particularly common among new college graduates and other inexperienced job-seekers. In most cases, employers are in business to make a profit. They want to know what you can do for their bottom line, not what they can do to fulfil your career dreams.

Leaving the Next Action with the Employer

Too many letters end with a line like this: 'If you are interested in my qualifications, please call me.' Proactive sales letters, in which the job-seeker requests an interview and promises to follow up with a phone call, are far more effective.

Using an Unprofessional Email Address

Roseybumcheeks@abc.com may have been a good idea when you registered your email account, but it will do you no favours when applying for a job. Always have an acceptable and professional email address that preferably includes your full name.

Using an Address Which Is Not Local

If you are from out of town, consider using a friend's address. Companies may use your location against you, either because the commute is too long or because they're worried you may not be able to relocate.

Making Your Sales Letter Too Long

As much as possible, keep your cover letter at one

page or just over. You need to become skilled at selling yourself as effectively and succinctly as possible. View your cover letter like an advertisement for yourself. The longer your letter, the less of a chance it has of being read. Remember you're writing for busy people. Help them and you'll help yourself.

Not proofreading your letter before sending it

Always check, re-check and check again when it comes to spelling and grammar. I suggest you check it and then ask someone else to look it over too. A good tip is to print your letter and then edit it. You'll often find errors on paper that you missed on screen.

When checking the content of your letter, read the letter out loud. When you do this, you'll often hear whether something 'sounds off' or doesn't flow logically. Problems we tend to miss when we just read with our eyes.

In the above chapter, I covered some common errors that you want to avoid when writing your own sales letter. In the next chapter, I'll cover some of the most frequently asked questions about cover/sales letters.

Chapter 11:

FREQUENTLY ASKED QUESTIONS

Below are some of the most frequently asked questions about writing cover/sales letters. Some of these are also answered in more depth elsewhere in this book. This is just a quick reference for your convenience.

Is a Cover Letter Necessary?

Unless you've been asked not to send one or you know that your particular field or job has an application process that doesn't require one then, yes! For the most part, a cover letter is expected. A colleague of mine told me he hardly ever reads cover letters because they all look and sound the same, but he won't even consider an application without one. The cover letter is your first opportunity to show the employer why and how you are the best fit for their needs.

How Long Should My Letter Be?

As long as it needs to be but definitely no more than one to two pages. The shorter you can make it without compromising the message, the better. Your cover letter is like your own personal advertisement in response to theirs. It needs to be concise, pithy and effective. Cut out all unnecessary words and 'fluff'.

What's The Most Important Part?

It's all important, but since your letter probably has just seconds to grab someone's attention, in my opinion the most important part is the first line. Is it different, captivating and intriguing? The first line will entice the reader to want to read more.

Will This Method Work Across All Industries?

It will for most but not for all. There are some types of jobs in some countries that require applications to follow a specific format. Having to do this may make it challenging to embrace this format completely. For instance those in the legal, academic and government fields but even for these you may still be able to apply some of the principles discussed in this book.

Is It Acceptable to Mass Produce the Same Letter If the Jobs Are Very Similar?

No two work places or jobs will ever be exactly the same and so no two letters should ever be exactly the same. You must tailor each letter to the company and positon you want.

Should I Write My Resume or Cover Letter First?

I don't think it matters. Do what feels best to you. Creating a resume is not within the scope of this book, but obviously you must have one tailored to the job you're applying for. Remember, your resume is an extension of your letter and one must support the other.

Should I Include References in My Cover Letter?

No. They don't belong here, or in your resume for that matter. They belong in the interview phase. You may say you have references available on request on your resume. Most companies won't check your references unless they're seriously interested in hiring you, and this won't be till later in the process.

Will This Method Work for All Levels of Jobs?

Yes, however it's important to remember that the content, style and tone of the letter may need to be altered for the level of job you are applying for. Once you understand the purpose of a cover letter as taught here, you can apply these principles to any level of job.

I'm Not Very Experienced. Will This Method Work for Me?

The more qualified and experienced you are, the easier it is to add value to any prospective job situation. If you have less experience, even if you are totally new to the job market, or if your experience is a bit diverse and skimpy because you've moved in and out of different jobs, then you'll have to show how you can still add value to the job you want.

In this case, look for transferrable skills and experience. You may have to think about your experience deeply and figure out how it'll apply to the job you're applying for. Sometimes experience and skills can first appear to be unrelated to the job at hand, but with some further thought can be applied in a creative way. For example, you may have no direct experience as a workshop facilitator, but you may be a very successful member of a Toastmasters club. How then can you draw from one to support the other?

Once you've figured out the connection, you may have to connect the dots for other people. For instance, if as a toastmaster you've had experience speaking in front of large audiences, then you could relate this to the workshop facilitator role, because it will also require you to be comfortable speaking in front of audiences.

How Should I Lay My Letter Out?

Typically, this should be laid out like any other business letter. But since this book may be read by people in different countries with different customs, I suggest you find out what local requirements are for your country and follow those. With that said, as long your letter appears professional, then it shouldn't matter too much if it doesn't follow custom completely.

Usually a business letter includes yours and the company's address, the date, and the subject of the letter. The subject might include the title or the reference number of the job you're applying for. To save space, I would write your own name and address across the top of the letter, perhaps in a different font or size or even bolded so it looks like a letterhead. Here's an example:

Heather Davis - 400 Box Rd, Miami Beach, Florida 33139 - PH (888) 305-9998 – hdavis@abcmail.com

I also think it's fine to use the name of the person and company but not include their full address, which will also help to save space. Here is an example:

John Boon

HR Manager, ABC Communications

Of course, if this isn't acceptable wherever you live, then you need to adapt your letter for local customs.

What Font Should I Use?

Stay with traditional fonts—Times New Roman, Arial, Verdana or Courier. Do not use multiple fonts in your letters.

Is There Anything I Should Definitely Avoid Including in My Letter?

Stay away from exclamation marks, smiley faces, other emoticons and colours.

Do You Have Any Tips for What to Put in The Subject Line of an Application Email?

Email is often the first point of contact between you and the person who will read the cover letter, so the subject line can make all the difference.

Keep it short and to the point by eliminating unnecessary words.

Example: Assistant Accountant Application

Put the most important information at the start of the subject line. According to litmus.com, 50% or more of emails are now read on mobile devices. A mobile phone only shows 24 to 30 characters of a subject line.

Example: Talent Acquisition Manager – 8 Years' Experience

Be clear about who you are and what you want. Don't use vague lines like 'my resume for you'. Instead specify which position you're applying for.

Example: Jill Box - IT Sales Role

Use keywords for search and filtering. If a hiring manager manages their email using filters, then you want to include words they might use to search for applications. The title of the position, job reference numbers and words like 'job application'.

If possible include the job title, any reference number provided and your name.

Example: Passport Officer, Ref XZ578K – Jane Smith Application

If you're qualified, you can also include acronyms after your name to help you stand out but only if they're relevant to the position.

Example: David Bean, PhD

If someone has referred you for the position, make sure you start the subject line with their name.

Example: Referred by Nancy Thomas for Editor Position

If you like to be different, you could try being creative. But be aware these more creative subject lines won't show up in searches and could even send your email directly to a spam folder.

Examples: Your next hire, From the world's greatest salesman (or substitute any role), Am I your next solution?, HR Exec looking for next role, Hiring me will change your company because . . .

Where Can I Find a List of Words to Help Me Write Achievement Statements?

I'm sure you can find these on the Internet, but here's my own list of action verbs, which I refer to when I write my own letters:

Adapted, administered, advised, analysed, applied, arranged, assisted, balanced, billed, briefed, carried out, communicated, compiled, completed, computed, conducted, controlled, coordinated, created, defined, delegated, delivered, demonstrated, designed, determined, developed, directed, doubled, earned, edited, eliminated, enabled, enforced, enhanced, established, evaluated, expanded, expedited, facilitated, filed, formed, fostered, founded, generated, guided, harnessed, illustrated, implemented, improved, increased, innovated, instructed, introduced, invented, launched, led, maintained, managed, mastered, mediated, monitored, negotiated, observed, operated, organized, participated, performed, persuaded, planned, prepared, presented, produced, programmed, provided, published, received, recommended, reduced, reorganized, reviewed, revised, scheduled, screened, selected, served, set up, sold, solved, streamlined, structured, supervised, supported, surpassed, surveyed, targeted, taught, teamed with, tested, trained, tripled, utilized, wrote

What If I Don't Have Any Achievements?

The problem with writing about your achievements is that, unless you did something extremely significant, you probably never thought about how your contribution made a difference in previous roles. See if you can come up with achievements that might not have been obvious at first. You could also ask your last manager to give you ideas.

You can learn a good lesson from this though. Keep track of your achievements while you're working and, more importantly, make an effort to stand out and you'll never be short of achievements for your next application.

How Does ATS Software Make Provision for Analysing More Creative Job Applications?

It doesn't. If you're in one of the arts industries like design or advertising, an ATS is incapable of evaluating your career history accurately, especially if you've had a long one. Applications for jobs like these often rely on a lot more than just text documents to demonstrate skills and talent. Make sure you read my final chapter where I introduce the idea of video cover letters.

How do I end my letter?

Nobody seems to be 100% certain how to end a letter. The two most common forms are 'Yours faithfully,' and 'Yours sincerely,'. I prefer 'faithfully', but the other way is fine too.

I've just covered most of the frequently asked questions about cover letters that I'm aware of. If you had a burning question you wanted answered, hopefully you found the answer in this chapter.

If you do have another question either now or in the future and you think the answer would benefit others, please either write to me at markbaker@thestandoutway.com or let me know in your review if you leave one.

Chapter 12:

WHAT'S NEXT?

In summary, if you want to write a stand out cover letter you must decide you want to stand out first. Next you must prepare to stand out which includes knowing why you're a stand out candidate. Finally you must market yourself by writing a letter of introduction which follows a sales letter format, one that's designed to stand out and grab the reader's attention. If you apply what you've learned in this book you'll already be well on your way to standing out from the masses. But why stop here? Why not take the principles you've learned and stand out even further? Let me explain.

I've already suggested you'll stand out if you follow two simple tips when it comes to the packaging and delivery of your letter. Always address your personalised letter to the person you want to read it and make sure your letter and resume are not separated if possible. But what if your cover letter wasn't a letter at all? What if instead of writing a letter you created a cover letter *video*, applying the same principles in this book? Do you think this would help you stand out? You bet it would.

Today some innovative companies are already requesting job applicants create cover letter videos. These organisations are the ones to watch. They're putting people back in their businesses because they've realized that regardless of technology they need the right people to make things work. Video cover letters give them a much clearer and faster idea of whether an applicant is right for them or not.

Obviously through the medium of video you'll be able to express your personality and individuality far beyond the limitations of the written word. This is also the ideal solution for those in more creative industries where ATS software is unable to capture an applicant's creative energy.

You may be shuddering at the thought though. So first you want me to be a salesperson and now you want me to look and sound good on camera too? Video cover letters may not be for everybody but don't dismiss them yet. Today it's quick and easy to produce effective, promotional videos without you ever having to feature as a live 'star'.

Reading about how to write stand out cover letters without ever actually creating one will never get you to interviews or get you hired in your dream job. You can only get better at this task by practising. The question is are you going to take the comfortable route, forget about what you've learned and go back to doing what you've always done? Or are you going to take action? It all begins with writing that first word.

By now you should know that we human beings are

odd creatures. We tend to know what we have to do, that we can do it and that we have the power to do it and yet we often still don't do it. Why don't we take action when we know that the action will move us to new heights? Usually new, unknown actions are uncomfortable, so we tend to avoid them. We often procrastinate when we don't have a clear, suitable goal, when we're not focused on what's required to be done, and when we don't have an action plan to follow.

If you're after a dream job, then you do have a goal. Decide right now that you're going to get that job and set a deadline for doing it. You have a detailed action plan —simply follow what this book teaches. Then attach your amazing cover letter to your just as amazing resume, press send and expect them to call you.

I'll leave you with this last bit of advice—stand out in life! If you're working only to pay bills, then you'll only do what's required and you won't grow. Consequently, you'll find writing cover letters more and more challenging because, although you'll have been busy working for many years, you won't have much to offer others. This means you'll have no option but to fall in with everybody else, all competing for the same boring jobs.

Don't stop growing. Use each job to help others and advance yourself so you're ready for each new chapter of your life. Stand out, be proud, be amazing, be different and your cover letters will be easy to write.

Did you enjoy reading this book?

If you did I'd appreciate it if you could leave me a review on Amazon.

Doing this provides me with feedback about why liked it and it helps others decide whether this is a book they would like to buy.

Thank you for taking the time to write a review.

About the Author

Mark Baker has unintentionally been showing people about how to write cover letters that stand out for years. His expert knowledge in this field has come from writing many cover letters himself and from being a hiring manager. He decided to write *Stand Out Cover Letters* to help more job seekers who are serious about what they do, to stand out in this way too.

Mark lives in Sydney, Australia. He spends his time helping individuals as well as businesses to beat procrastination, get what they want and stand out above the crowd. If you would like to know more about Mark and his work, please write to him at markbaker@thestandoutway.com

Made in the USA
Columbia, SC
18 August 2017